We're that famous hidden place
MisterO1
Extraordinary Pizza
We're that famous hidden place
www.misterO1.com
MisterO1
Extraordinary Pizza
We're that famous hidden place
MisterO1
Extraordinary Pizza
Dine in - Take out - Delivery
www.misterO1.com

Mister O1
Mister O1
Extraordinary
Pizza

PIZZA
VISIONARY

UPPONE

PIZZA VISIONARY

THE JOURNEY TO AN EXTRAORDINARY BRAND

1680
Mister O1
Extraordinary Pizza

CHEF RENATO VIOLA

G Editions G New York

First published in 2025 by

G Editions

www.geditions.com

media@geditions.com

First edition, 2025

Library of Congress Cataloging-in-Publication data is available from the publisher.

Hardcover edition

ISBN: 978-1-943876-67-9

Printed and bound in China

10 9 8 7 6 5 4 3 2 1

MIX
Paper | Supporting responsible forestry
FSC® C144853
FSC www.fsc.org

CUPPONE

Individuals with
To qualify for an
the beneficiary
ability by

1680
Mister O1
Extraordinary
Pizza
nary ability.
in the US,
strate extraordinary
al or international acclaim.
Pe
il beneficia
supportate c
adidas

Mister 01

CONTENTS

CUPPONE 1963

1680
Mister O1
Extraordinary
Pizza

INTRODUCTION

We Started as a Pizzeria and Now We are a Brand.

The story of Mister O1 begins with a hidden pizzeria inside a nondescript office building on a side street of Miami's famous Lincoln Road. The space was a modest 640 square feet. There were 9 tables and seating for 18 (sometimes we could squeeze in 30). People thought we would close in 6 months; we just celebrated our 10 year anniversary. And from this small-but-mighty location, a pizza empire was born, spawning 8 corporate locations, a pizza school, a commissary kitchen, and 13 franchise locations from Florida to Texas and beyond.

Many people thought we were crazy. Many people thought we would not succeed. I perform best when faced with a challenge. When I can prove the impossible to be possible, I give 1,000 percent. I have been competitive since I was a kid. Opening a place of my own has been my dream, and with my team, I have created something extraordinary. This is our story.

As a teenager in Italy, I was captivated by the reality show *Miami Ink*, set in the vibrant locale of South Beach. Little did I know then that Miami would become the canvas for *my* dreams. Now, years later, it's surreal to count Ami James, one of the show's tattoo artists, among our regular guests at Mister O1—a full-circle moment indeed. Miami isn't just where I chased my aspirations; it's where I've planted roots, forged lasting bonds, and nurtured a brand.

Life came full circle again in our collaboration with Miguel Blatt, a former boss from my early days at Dolce restaurant, now a valued district manager within our team. Miguel is set to become our inaugural franchisee in Georgia—an achievement that fills me with pride. It speaks volumes about our ability to attract top talent and provide avenues for growth.

Domenico D'Anna, known as "Mimmo," who worked with me at Dolce and is now a franchise owner in Melbourne, Florida, echoes these sentiments eloquently: "South Beach holds a special place in our hearts. It's where it all began—the essence captured by the number 1680 on our logo, marking the address of our inaugural location. Though we've outgrown our 'hidden gem' status, we remain committed to the core values that made us special—a sense of intimacy, community, and delivering exceptional experiences."

In essence, Mister O1 has evolved from a humble pizzeria into a recognized brand, yet our essence remains unchanged—a testament to our unwavering commitment to authenticity and excellence.

South Beach holds a special place in our hearts. It's where it all began.

1680
MICHIGAN
FOOD&WINE
The Best Pizza in Every State
Florida

MISTER 01 BY THE NUMBERS

1.7 million Total pizzas made annually across all locations.

450,000 Annual pizzas produced at corporate-only locations.

250,000 Number of Nutella pizzas (page 133) crafted yearly across all outlets, making Mister 01 the largest Nutella consumer on the East Coast.

91,000 Antipasti plates served annually across all establishments.

54,711 Total Nutella pizzas (page 133) and calzones served across all locations.

400 Average number of delivery pizzas dispatched daily from the Brickell location.

300 Daily covers at the South Beach location during its inaugural year.

250 Number of complimentary chocolate croissants gifted to guests daily at the South Beach outlet.

120 Maximum pizzas per hour churned out by the oven at the South Beach establishment.

19 Tables present in the original South Beach location.

7 Employees at the inaugural South Beach location.

28in x 25in Standard dimensions of every table at Mister 01.

Mister 01
TIME FOR EXTRAORDINARY PIZZA

CHAPTER 1

THE 01 VISA

AN AMERICAN DREAM

We signed the lease for our first location in April 2014, but the story starts months earlier. I was working the pizza station at Dolce Italian, a restaurant in the Gale Hotel, South Beach. My future business partner's father, Andrea Mascagni, whom we now call the "Leader," frequently dined there. He persistently suggested that I should team up with his son, Umberto, who had recently moved to Miami and held a business degree.

Umberto, now affectionately known as the "President," became a regular at Dolce. We eventually became friends, playing basketball together in South Beach and hanging out after work. Umberto believed in my talent, and together we decided to open a pizza restaurant. But first, we needed a space and funds.

One day, I visited my lawyer's office on the seventh floor of a building at 1680 Michigan Ave. On the ground floor, hidden inside the lobby, was a sushi restaurant with a lease sign. From the street, there was no indication of a restaurant inside; it looked like a typical office building. You had to know it was there to find it. This location was the opposite of South Beach's flashy scene, and it seemed counterintuitive for first-time restaurateurs. Yet, I showed Umberto the space, and somehow, he believed in the vision.

"We wanted to do something different: high-quality pizza at a reasonable price with extraordinary service."

We felt people would come regardless of the location if we offered excellence.

Umberto explains, "If you have a quality product, people will find you. I loved the idea of a speakeasy–something only locals knew about. It was risky, but I was always confident in our plan."

We wanted to do something different: high-quality pizza at a reasonable price with extraordinary service.

Co-founders Umberto Mascagni and Renato Viola at the South Beach location, where the Mister O1 journey began.

With a meager budget of $180,000 (today, a new restaurateur in South Beach would need at least $1 million), we set about making our vision a reality. We invested in new floors, quality furniture, and a fully equipped kitchen. Our goal was to create a warm, clean, and inviting space where people would feel at home. We named our place Visa-O1, after the work visa reserved for those with "extraordinary ability" that allowed me to move to America and pursue my dream. This name perfectly encapsulated our ethos.

Mimmo recalls those early days; "I've known Chef Renato since our time together at Dolce. I was on the front-of-house team, and he was the pizza chef. Being from Naples, Italy, we bonded with other Italians at Dolce, always having fun and joking around. Renato did the job of two to three pizza makers by himself. Our pizza sales at Dolce soared, thanks to his incredible skills. He even introduced the star pizza there, gaining a reputation on social media. We participated in Bravo TV's Best New Restaurant competition hosted by Tom Colicchio, and we won in 2015. That was a great experience for the whole team.

"After leaving Dolce, Renato showed me the new space. He brought me to a side street and into an office building. When I saw the original space, I felt the love and passion that went into it. Despite the small budget, the attention to detail was impeccable, from the tables to the kitchen and pizza station design. It was as if they built it with their own hands. I told Renato, 'You're underestimating how successful this place will be. It's too small.'"

We opened in October 2014, working seven days a week, often twenty hours a day. We even have pictures of me sleeping on flour bags between shifts. My wife, Manuela Faniglione, believed in this small venture and helped from the beginning, doing whatever was needed—answering phones, working the register, and more. Now, she heads our human resources department. Manuela recalls, "I knew the first place would be a success. I was

TOP: Chef Renato crafting pizzas at Dolce in the Gale Hotel.
BOTTOM: Chef Renato in the kitchen at the Mister O1 South Beach location.

1680
MICHIGAN

Umberto and Renato standing in front of the first Mister O1 van—originally Visa O1—that was used to deliver dough and supplies to the Brickell and Wynwood locations.

sure, even though it was small and hidden. I believe in Renato—he's focused, and I support his unconventional choices. I knew it was a success when he started sleeping there!"

We soon became known as the "hidden place" for authentic, swoon-worthy Italian pizza. My pizza style blends Italian thin crust with a New York–style quality, ensuring it remains crisp and not soggy in the middle.

Initially, we spent nothing on marketing and had minimal social media presence—our reputation grew entirely by word of mouth. The tenants of the office building were our first promoters. A *Miami New Times* article and a *Deco Drive* interview soon followed. In January 2015, writer Carina Ost declared in the *New Times*, "Pizza in a hidden location just tastes better." She described the allure of our secret gem inside the office building off Lincoln Road. "The kitchen door opens, and the aroma of freshly tossed dough and cooked pizza seeps out. We are told it will be a few minutes for a table. The smells are alluring, with '50s rock 'n' roll playing in the background and patrons speaking beautiful Italian. This place is legit."

During those early years, there were times when fifty guests waited to dine in the lobby, sometimes for over an hour and a half. People would walk along Lincoln Road and then return. After six months of this craziness, we decided to implement a reservation system (we've since reverted to a waitlist policy). We were handling three hundred covers a day, open from 11:30 a.m. to 11 p.m. Meetings were held in the back kitchen by the dishwasher, with our lawyer sitting on crates. A year later, we got a desk, then two desks, then an office in a co-working space. We stored sodas and products under the desks due to a lack of proper storage.

We never acquired a liquor license, sticking to beer and wine, a policy we maintain to this day. The same goes for pasta and gelato—we don't offer them. The answer is always the same: I am a pizza chef, and this is what we do. As our reputation grew, we opened more locations and franchises, but we have remained consistent in our commitment to high-quality pizza, reasonable prices, and extraordinary service.

Throughout it all, we remained local-driven. Tourists from around the world soon discovered our hidden gem. Our reputation for high-quality, authentic Italian pizza with exceptional service spread rapidly. The small, hidden pizzeria on a side street became the foundation for a growing empire, and we knew we had something truly special.

ABOVE: The Mister O1 Aventura team in training ahead of their grand opening in 2022.
BELOW: Chef Renato and Ana, a dedicated server who has been part of the team for over seven years."

EXIT

IN THE BEGINNING

THINGS WE DID NOT HAVE WHEN OPENING:

- A business plan.
- A reservation system.
- A cocktail menu (we still don't have one; we only serve beer and wine).
- An office space.
- A marketing team or a marketing plan.
- A freezer (we still don't have one; everything is fresh).
- Market research.

CHAPTER 2

FROM MAESTRO TO MISTER

MY BACKGROUND IN ITALY

My journey from "Maestro" to Mister—from apprentice to champion—begins in Southern Italy, where I grew up immersed in the kitchen. The kitchen was our world: we played, watched TV, and did our homework there. No one ever sat on the couch in the living room. From the age of four, I would help my mom make ragu sauce on Sunday mornings. One Sunday, she made pizza dough, and from that moment, I was hooked. I would cry on the Sundays she didn't make dough, begging her to please make pizza.

When I turned eleven, I started spending weekends at professional pizzerias, helping out and observing the pizza makers at work. My tasks weren't always exciting—one summer, I spent my days hauling a wheelbarrow filled with wood for the pizza oven—but I was eager to learn. Throughout my childhood, I worked at pizzerias on weekends, studying with the "maestros."

In Italy, a "maestro" of pizza is someone who has a passion for their work, uses the best-quality ingredients, and possesses a deep knowledge of technique and tradition. But as I learned from the maestros, I noticed they often relied on tradition rather than understanding. For example, I'd ask, "Why don't you mix the yeast with the salt?" The answer was always, "Because this is the way it was taught to me." Or I'd ask, "How much salt should we add to the dough?" And the answer would be, "When your water tastes like ocean water."

I found this unsatisfying. I always wanted to learn more. I wanted to know the "why" and the "how"—how do all these ingredients work together? More importantly, how does the science of ingredients affect the dough? So, I started traveling and studying more formally. Just as lawyers and doctors study for their professions, I believed I should study mine.

Chef Renato showcasing his skills in pizza acrobatics as a member of the Italian Pizza Acrobatics Team.

30

"Pizza Fantasia"
2° Classificato
bergiornale

API
Associazione
Pizzerie
Italiane
6° Campionato Naz.le di Pizza
Trofeo "Poggia Pizza"
Fiuggi 2006
Acrobatica a Squadre
1° Classificata

If you have knowledge, you can improve, and I'm always trying to improve.

I took courses to study the chemistry of ingredients and learned why certain things create the chemical reactions that give dough its shape, elasticity, and texture. I traveled through Italy to study the different styles of pizzas. Each region has its own type of pizza; you can travel just twenty minutes to a different city, and it will have a unique style and flavor. Over time, I developed my own style of pizza and created my own techniques with the dough.

To become Chef Renato, I sacrificed my teenage years. From fourteen to twenty-eight, I was always working, honing my skills. My travels were always for work, for competitions. While my friends saved money for Italian scooters at fifteen, I used my earnings to buy my first spiral mixer to make my own dough. At twenty, I started training for the Acrobatic competition, and from then on, my career took off. But I have no regrets because I wouldn't be where I am now without that dedication. Like any goal in life, you have to train for it every day.

OPPOSITE: Chef Renato competing and receiving prestigious awards across Europe. BELOW: Chef Renato's first competition win, held in Silvi Marina, Abruzzo, Italy. Representing his home region of Campania, he won with his remarkable creation, the 2005 pizza.

AWARDS AND RECOGNITION

FOOD&WINE

The Best Pizza in Every State

By David Landsel
Published on April 28, 2021

Florida

[...There are plenty of Europeans who wished they lived in Florida—some of them are making moves to do just that—and the odds are good that a few of them are Italians who will open pizzerias, or at least that is how it seems these days.

All apologies to the Northeast pie guys trading on their heritage down here, but when you want the best, just go somewhere they speak Italian, the modern kind, like **Mister O1 in Miami**, named for the O-1 Visa granted to **Renato Viola**, a well-regarded pizza maker from the old country who came to the United States because some very smart person in government decided we needed his pizza skills.

From humble beginnings, the restaurant has grown to five locations in the region—the better for everyone to have access to Viola's delicious and distinctive star-cornered pies, with pockets of creamy ricotta cheese...]

https://www.foodandwine.com/travel/restaurants/best-pizza-every-state

MISTER O1:

- *Food & Wine Magazine* – Named "The Best Pizza in Every State" (2021)
- *Michelin Guide* – Recommended in 2022 & 2023 (South Beach location)
- *Barstool Sports* – 8.9 rating by Dave Portnoy (2021)
- *The Infatuation* – Listed among the Best Restaurants in Brickell
- *Ocean Drive Magazine* – Featured in "Best Burrata Dishes in Miami"
- *Miami New Times* – Winner of "Best Pizza" Readers' Choice (2021 & 2023)
- *Best of Miami-Dade Magazine* – Named "Best Pizza" (2023)
- *Google Reviews* – 4.8+ rating at all locations
- *PMQ Pizza Magazine* – Named "#1 Most Popular Independent Pizzeria in America"

CHEF RENATO

- *World Pizza Championship* – Winner of "Best Pizza" for the Star Luca (page 107)
- *Pizza Marketplace* – Recognized in the Movers & Shakers 2023 list, Top 25 Executives category

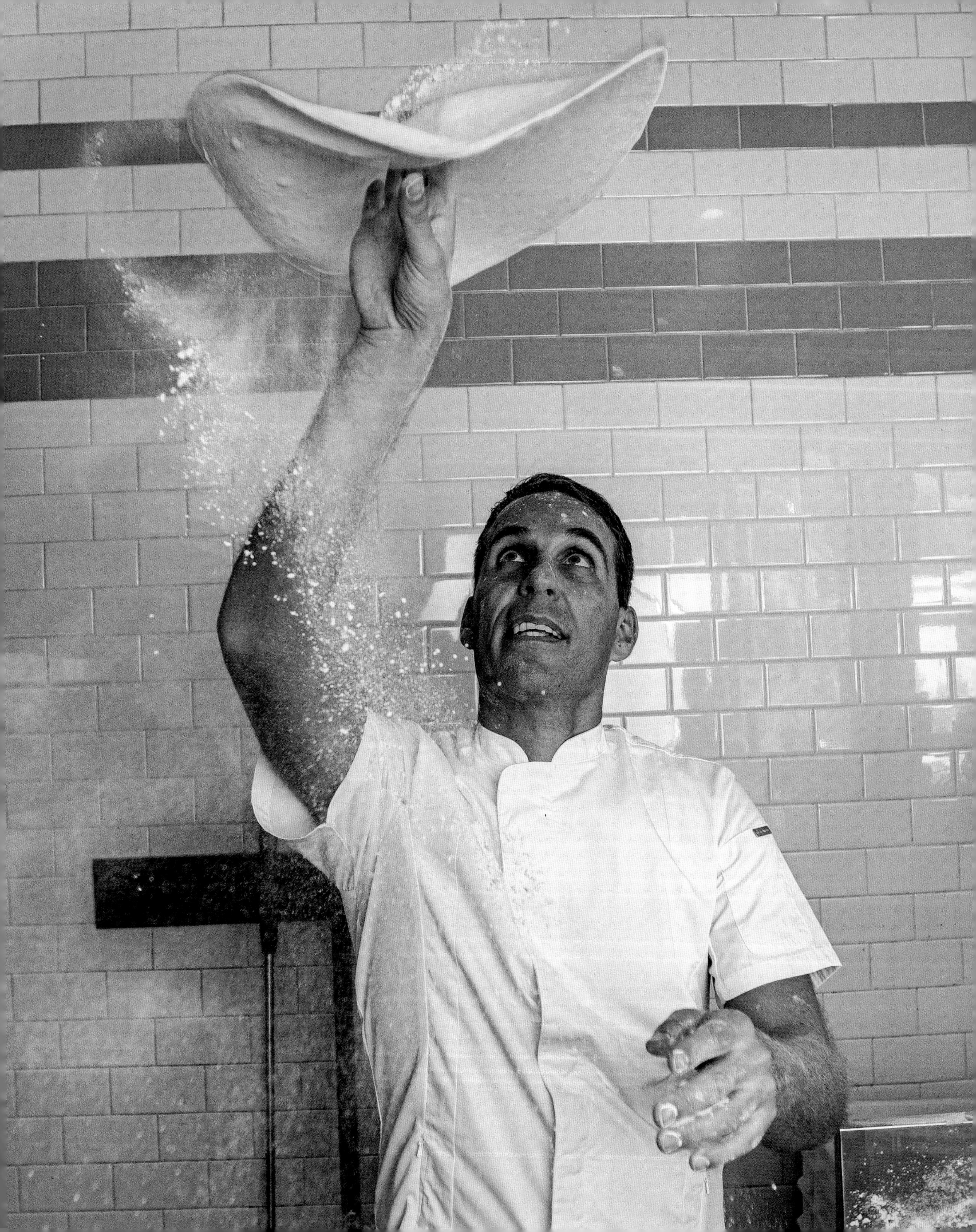

CHAPTER 3

A STAR IS BORN

THE STORY BEHIND THE STAR PIZZA

In 2008, I created the Star Pizza for a competition in Monaco. This was the most significant competition for me at the time, as the finale (with only twenty finalists) took place in Monte Carlo, with all travel expenses covered—naturally, everyone wanted to participate. The judging criteria were based on creativity, taste, and the menu you've developed.

I was searching for something quick to execute, something that would only take a few minutes to prepare. I came up with the idea of a combination between a calzone and a pizza. It was a simple proposition: eight slits are cut into the edge of stretched dough. A slice of salami topped with a hefty swirl of ricotta is placed on each of the eight points. Then, the dough is folded over like a paper airplane, creating eight small dough pockets that ooze rich ricotta cheese into a center of tangy San Marzano tomato sauce.

I submitted the recipe with a drawing. Nearly ten thousand recipes were entered into the competition. And boom! I got selected for the semifinals in Milan, narrowing down to only one hundred chefs, whose originators were invited to Milan. Later, twenty-five were brought to Monaco to cook their creations. I had never actually made it before arriving in Monaco. The first rendition was topped with ingredients common on the Cilento Coast, which surrounds Agropoli: mozzarella di bufala, ultra-dense dried salami, porcini mushrooms, and the smoked-and-dried mozzarella called scamorza. At twenty-two years old, I was one of the three finalists.This was the true beginning of my journey and allowed me the opportunity to receive the O1 Visa and travel to America.

Now, the Star Pizza is replicated by many other places, but it doesn't bother me. I remember what my grandmother always said: "It's better to be copied than to copy others."

I came up with the idea of a combination between a calzone and a pizza.

Chef Renato at the Pizza World Championship in Monte Carlo, where he achieved the prestigious "Best Pizza" award for his iconic creation, the Star Luca (page 107).

The Star Pizza is not just one thing—there are about five or six elements that have to come together to make the star itself.

First, the dough needs to be at room temperature—we leave it out for an hour. This helps us get the color, size, and texture that we are looking for.

Then, the rolled-out dough has to be a perfect circle. Next, we make little cuts—eight cuts—and they have to be perfectly spaced out. The amount of sauce and cheese is also important—if it gets too wet, then the ricotta slides out of the pocket. With the right amount of sauce, the ricotta stays in the pocket. Also, the ricotta shouldn't be sitting out too long; the fats get soft, and it needs to be cold.

During the baking process, we make sure to rotate the pizza to ensure it cooks evenly. It takes an average of five to six minutes to cook—slightly longer than a regular pizza to account for the extra moisture in the ricotta.

When it's cooked, I'm looking for the color on the points to be a nice cappuccino brown—that's when you know it's done.

Star Luca: The first star-shaped pizza created by Chef Renato, earning him the World Pizza Championship and now a signature item on the Mister O1 menu (page 107).

LEAD BY EXAMPLE

The Star Pizza is not just one thing—there are about five or six elements that have to come together to make the star itself.

Chef Renato preparing the Star Luca, carefully filling its points with ricotta before sealing them (page 107).

The Star Pizza is replicated by many other places, but I remember what my grandmother always said: "It's better to be copied than to copy others."

MASTER CHEF

CHAPTER 4

BEYOND THE "HIDDEN PLACE"

OUR EXPANDING LOCATIONS

We didn't open with a business plan. We don't believe in that. Our "business plan" is: work hard and work harder. We created our business plan not in an office but in the kitchen. Perhaps our revenue would be higher if we sold cocktails in addition to beer and wine, but I believe in simplicity. I believe that the best combination with pizza is beer or wine, so that's what we do. We are not motivated by revenue or "the bottom line"—we are motivated by doing what we can do in the best way possible. The money is a consequence of our hard work.

Eventually, we decided to expand beyond South Beach. Wynwood was supposed to be our second location. We signed the lease in March 2015, not even one year into our first location in South Beach, but we believed in our concept. The reason behind our third opening, which

We are driven by a commitment to excellence in everything we do.

BELOW: The Coconut Grove back-of-house team.

2311
www.visao1.com
Visa-01
Extraordinary
Pizza
COMING SOON!
2311

1680
Mister O1
Extraordinary
Pizza
We're that famous hidden place
2315
PIZZA SCHOOL
ART
OF MAKING
LOVE FOR
EATING
EXTRAORDINARY
PIZZA

The Wynwood location in the final stages of preparation before its opening.

finally took place in October 2017, is largely attributed to construction challenges and misplaced trust in certain individuals. At the time, Wynwood was not as expensive as it is now. We found a space that was 3,300 square feet, so we decided to build a larger commissary kitchen to produce the dough in larger batches. We got a private loan and partnered with someone to do construction, but that turned out to be a mistake. We lost about 80 percent of the capital we had on unreliable construction. It was a big blow for us. But we pulled our resources together to continue. We ended up getting a second private loan to finish the project and were able to pay it back in two years instead of seven, which is a testament to our success.

Amid all the drama with the Wynwood location, we took the opportunity to open a Brickell location. One thing you must understand about us at the time was that we were South Beach people. I lived on West Avenue and used to ride a scooter or bicycle to work. I wasn't familiar with Brickell, but Carlos Galan, one of our guests and the owner of Dolores But You Can Call Me Lolita, a very popular restaurant in Brickell, liked our pizza and approached us about opening in the space underneath Dolores. It was a small space but in a busy location with a lot of pedestrian traffic and apartment buildings nearby. To this day, we remain close with him. He's a hospitality professional; we learned a lot from him, and he always gives us good recommendations and feedback.

As Umberto says, the location was great, right in the center of Brickell. The deal was a little risky for us—it was percentage rent with a minimum payment of $20,000, which was high for us at the time, but we said, "Let's do it." Again, we did zero marketing, we covered the windows, did the renovation, and opened with no fanfare.

We opened in October 2016, exactly two years after our first location. And from the start, we had a line every day, a waiting list of people waiting for tables. Again, with Brickell, we kept it small—only 21 tables, all of them two-tops, and always in the dimensions of 28 by 25 inches. These tables are easily combined for larger parties.

One week after we opened the Brickell location, we received a letter—a somewhat friendly letter—from a "big credit card company" with the same name, telling us we had to change our name, as it infringed on the company's trademark. People in their headquarters heard about us, which is kind of incredible considering we were just a small pizzeria, and they felt we had to change the name. So we went to a trademark lawyer who reviewed everything and advised us to change the name. Some of our guests had already been calling me "Mister O1," so we kept all the branding and font style and changed it to "Mister O1 Extraordinary Pizza." It was the best decision we made. We feel this is a better name, and it's more recognizable now.

In January 2017, the *Miami Herald* wrote a story about the situation, calling out the company by name, which made our lawyer nervous. But in the end, the article gave us more exposure, and people came to support us as small business owners dealing with a big corporate company.

In Brickell, we were able to open with two ovens, whereas in South Beach, we only had one oven, which can produce 120 pizzas an hour, so we gave priority to the dining room and standby on the delivery. But in Brickell, we could perform well in both the dining room and delivery. After a year, we realized two ovens were not enough, so we added a third oven when we moved to our new Brickell location in March 2023. This was a bigger space in the back of Mary Brickell Village—again, hidden, just how we like it—but a bigger space, which was a challenge we accepted. This space has thirty-nine tables; I could put

OPPOSITE, TOP: The original Brickell location bustling on a lively weekend night.
OPPOSITE, BOTTOM: Outdoor seating at the new Brickell location in Mary Brickell Village, which opened in March 2023, featuring expanded seating and a modern design.

We are that famous hidden place
Mister O1
Extraordinary Pizza

PIZZA, SALADS & BURRATA BAR

two hundred seats, but I don't do it, because we like to keep things small. Why do we like to keep things small? Because we like to provide a personal experience. There might be a long waiting list for a table, but there's always fast service. Now it's full—we have tables outside, a nice plaza, and everything is constantly at capacity.

We were able to open Wynwood in October of 2017—three years after opening our first location in South Beach. But it was not without some drama. One week before we were slated to open, we received the news that a tropical storm was approaching. This ended up being Hurricane Irma, which made landfall in Florida—hitting the Florida Keys—on September 10, 2017, as a Category 4 hurricane. It then moved up to Central Florida, but Miami still sustained major rainfall, wind,

ABOVE: The interior of the new Brickell location in Mary Brickell Village.

There might be a long waiting list for a table, but there's always fast service.

Outdoor seating at the Coconut Grove location, situated within the vibrant CocoWalk Plaza.

and flooding. Many people, including myself and my family, decided to leave Miami and drive to Atlanta as the storm was predicted to be one of the worst Miami would experience and major destruction was anticipated. When the storm hit, we could see on the news that the neighborhood of Brickell was underwater from intense flooding, and we worried about our business. Remember—we had invested almost everything into the Wynwood location. So we were worried about losing everything. I was watching the news constantly from Atlanta.

When the storm was over, Pres walked over the Venetian causeway by foot to check the damage. Luckily, both the Brickell and Wynwood locations did not sustain much damage, and we were able to clean things up and reopen. But when we opened this Wynwood location, we had almost nothing in our account—we invested everything in this opportunity. But with the opening of Wynwood, our brand got more exposure, and people started to approach us and ask to partner or open their own locations.

In January 2021, in the midst of the COVID-19 pandemic, we opened our fourth location in the quaint neighborhood of Coconut Grove. Again, I knew nothing about Coconut Grove, but we were interested in the new redevelopment of Cocowalk. We saw that we had a lot of guests coming from Pinecrest, so we started to listen to the community and decided to open in Coconut Grove to be closer to our guests in South Miami. We knew we had a good delivery market there, so we thought we'd open our smallest location yet. But when we opened, we were so busy that we decided not to do deliveries to prioritize quality and meet the Mister O1 standards of taking care of the dining room first.

We have forty seats, and what's nice about this location is the outdoor plaza has common tables, so you can order takeout and enjoy the tables outside. Coconut Grove is a family place—the takeout window was very busy with families coming for quick meals to sit in the courtyard. In hindsight, we wish we could have rented a larger space since the community has embraced us so much.

Since then, we've opened more locations, including Aventura Park Square in March 2022, Bay Harbor Islands in October 2023, and Pinecrest and Doral in 2024. In each of these openings, we grow as a team and build our connection with the community. When you have the love of the community, it's everything.

BELOW: Exterior facade of the Pinecrest location, opened in June 2024.
OPPOSITE: Exterior facade and seating of the Aventura location, opened in March 2022.

Mister
109

S.PELLEGRINO

TOP: Outdoor seating at the Bay Harbor Islands location, opened in October 2023.

Mister 01

THE PIZZA SCHOOL

Creating our pizza school is another way we connect with our community.

When we were designing the Wynwood location, we didn't want to show the pizzeria from the street; we wanted to keep that element of secrecy. We liked the high ceilings of the space and wanted to keep them, so we created a small corridor in the front entrance and a glass-enclosed room with windows facing the street. The restaurant is still somewhat "hidden," but now there's a gallery in front, and we needed to create something there. My wife recommended that I have a hobby, so we created the pizza school. "People love to learn his techniques," says Manuela. "And he really wants people to go home and be able to make the pizza on their own. He likes to impart his knowledge to them."

Guests attending a Pizza School class in Texas.

A group of guests from Pizza School classes held in Texas and Miami.

SCHOOL

PIZZA SCHOOL

Martha
Marta

We like that the pizza school is visible from the street, and the pizzeria is hidden inside. It gets people curious, and they stop to watch the pizza tossing in action. The pizza school was also born out of the fact that a lot of people ask, "What's your secret?" They think it's the sauce, but it's not the sauce. Sure, our sauce is great; there's no sugar and no additives in it. But really, if anything is our secret, it's our flour, which is a special mixture of mineral and protein. So the pizza class shares the secret, the process, how to make the dough from scratch. People get an opportunity to stretch the dough, drink some wine and beer, connect with each other, and meet new people. The first year, we hosted more than one thousand people in the classes. Now we have a second chef who teaches the pizza classes with me. And we do private classes. So now we have a team dedicated to taking care of the pizza school. It is yet another way that we connect with our guests and give them an extraordinary experience.

Miami Pizza School, located at the Wynwood location.

PIZZA SCHOOL
TAYLOR

CHAPTER 5

BUILDING A TEAM

LESSONS IN HOSPITALITY

Lesson #1: Pizza is a Community Business. The Feeling is the Most Important Part.

Why do people love Mister O1? Perhaps it's because they don't expect a certain level of service from a pizzeria. We deliver an experience—we smile, we talk with the guests. Everyone gives a bit of energy to the guests. I tell my staff: your goal is not to sell more, but to sell right. Our guests say we are a safe place; we are consistent. The guests know they'll receive good customer service, a good atmosphere, and value. We have guests coming five times a week.

Once we found a way to be consistent with the pizza, we wanted to be consistent with the service. We are a people-driven company. We started with seven employees at our first location, and now we have grown to five hundred team members. We still have employees who started on day one and have stayed with us. It is also a family business. My wife joined the team after three months. There's also Grace Herrera, who started as a personal assistant and is now vice president of operations, involved in all decisions, and she's been with us for eight years.

Chef Renato with members of the training team at the opening of the Bay Harbor Islands location.

In the early days, each of us had ten positions. I was a pizza chef in charge of dough production, management, scheduling, inventory and marketing; sometimes I even delivered pizzas. When we only had South Beach and Brickell locations, we had to make the dough for both locations in South Beach. Every morning at 7 a.m., we'd make 1,500 balls of dough per day with a small spiral mixer that could mix a 55-pound (25-kilogram) bag of flour, finishing at 11 a.m. Then we'd go with a truck and bring it to Brickell, distributing it ourselves. Now things have changed, but I'm still wearing many hats. I always believe you have to give value to your time and see

MisterO1
109
WELCOME
MisterO1
Extraordinary
Pizza
MISTERO1.COM

THANKS FOR
5 YEARS OF

TIME FOR
PIZZA

We're in the people business, working side by side as one team—together, always on the same side.

FACING PAGE, TOP: Chef Renato with the back-of-house team at the South Beach location.
FACING PAGE, BOTTOM: Chef Renato with Carlos Medina, General Manager of the Naples and Fort Lauderdale locations, and Valentina García, Operating Partner of the Boynton Beach location.

where you can bring more value to the brand. So now I can give more value not on the line, but of support to the front of the house and back of the house.

According to Manuela, the reason we have flourished is because Umberto (Mister O1's president) and I (Mister O1's chef) work well together.. "The secret to their success? They have a good business partnership," says Manuela. "They're very different people, but they are united in their focus. They take care of the business like it's their home. Even when they are doing hard work, they are having fun—like when they used to have to drive the truck to deliver the dough to the locations, they would be playing around, honking the horn and being funny. Even now, they are very competitive; they play foosball in the office and they're always joking around."

We are in the people business. My staff is not "behind me"—we are on the same side. Over the years, I have learned you have to believe in other people and let them go. You can't micromanage too much. You have to let people make mistakes. We look for people with good energy and attitude. We look for people who show that hospitality is their lifestyle. Every position is important here. I always go to speak to the dishwasher because value them as I do the general manager. You know when people understand how important the dishwashers are? When they don't show up!

Manuela points out that a typical team member here needs to be able to roll with changes—because we change a lot. "We're always improving, we're always developing new systems for being faster and better. For example, we introduce new items on the menu and they need to prepare themselves for that. Or, for example, we started using QR codes for things so they need to learn that. We have servers who have been here for over five years, and in that time there have been plenty of changes, but they've all been able to adapt."

Chef Renato and Alfredo Keri, Boca Raton Operating Partner, during the pre-opening of the Mission Bay location.

CUPPONE

Lesson #2: The Customer is Not Always Right, but We Must Treat Them as if They Are.

Mimmo has seen our growth in the front-of-house team and explains: "From the very beginning when opening in South Beach, he was very customer-oriented. Most chefs are only focused on what is happening on the plates, but he cares about what is happening all around the restaurant—he has a 360-degree view. He cares about how the guests are feeling. It's what I want from a dining experience. I always think, if I'm a guest, how would I like to be treated? Do I want someone to wash the floor while I'm eating? No, I want to have my full experience. I want to be treated with respect by my server; I don't want to be pressured to order expensive wine or have a server upsell to me. I want a place I can go with my family twice a week."

Karif Cohen, Dr. Phillips Operating Partner, with guests at the Mission Bay location opening.

When it comes to service, tourists are the same as locals—we treat everyone like they're coming to our house and they remember us. In the beginning in South Beach, we would send tourists something on the house—like freshly made Nutella croissants for dessert—and this was surprising to the team, because they would say, "Chef, why would you do this? These people are from another country; they are not locals," and it's because we felt we had to treat them like locals, like they will come back. And they do. People come back whenever they are here on vacation and word spreads. They tell us, "My friends in Australia said we have to come to Mister O1 when we visit Miami." Now, when I travel, I always wear something that says Mister O1, and I get travelers telling me they recognize the name.

Social media is also an extension of hospitality. After all, a guest entering the restaurant should be treated as if they're entering my home. And if someone takes the time to write something about us, it's our duty to answer

1680
Extraordinary
Pizza
Naples
FOLLOW US AT @MISTERO1PIZZA
TIME FOR EXTRAORDINARY PIZZA

Exterior of the Mizner location, the first Mister O1 in Boca Raton, Florida.

them. Our standard is not to drop below 4.8 on Google reviews. We're always checking, always keeping tabs on our ratings. Even when we see a four-star review, we are alarmed—we think: what can we do? How can we improve? And we share with our staff the good—and sometimes the bad—reviews. They understand that in the time they give to their guests, they're giving value.

In the beginning, we did not have a social media or PR team. But we gained momentum with the star pizza, so we created a marketing team, helping the brand reach new guests, and the marketing supports the franchisees. Our job is to make sure our guests come back. And 99 percent of people are coming back. We need to leave them with a memory. That feeling is everything.

4.9 ★★★★★ 3,873 Google reviews

Boca Raton

4.9 ★★★★★ 5,208 Google reviews

Brickell

4.9 ★★★★★ 6,055 Google reviews

Coconut Grove

4.9 ★★★★★ 2,403 Google reviews

Grapevine

4.9 ★★★★★ 1,999 Google reviews

Lake Mary

4.9 ★★★★★ 3,786 Google reviews

Melbourne

4.9 ★★★★★ 2,592 Google reviews

Turtle Creek

4.9 ★★★★★ 7,816 Google reviews

Wynwood

Chef Renato with Manny, a friend and guest of Mister O1, during a Pizza School class.

Lesson #3: A Dream Without Goals is Just a Dream.

We are driven by our goals at Mister O1, yet we're also realists. Is pizza-making a craft? Absolutely, but it's not the whole picture. Hospitality is essential, as is a deep understanding of business acumen to ensure success.

Now the role of the pizza chef is changing. You can't just stay in the kitchen; you need to talk with the guests, you have to make sure they have a good experience.

Today, as a chef-owner, you have to be a good chef, who knows a little bit about accounting, HR, etc. You need to have a strong team around you. My dream was to open my own restaurant, but along the way, I also learned to be flexible and to trust my team.

Grace echoes this sentiment when she describes the strength of our team. "I would take this team to the moon," says Grace. "We all are working towards a shared goal and we've bought into this concept. And the shared passion has spread into the company. The respect comes from the top down. Our leadership passes their energy onto the team. We believe in it because our leadership believes in it."

Coconut Grove was one of our best openings. People had so much energy to give to the brand; they were ready to go back to work. The opening was perfect—the team, the machine, the vibe. It was my first opening where I was a little more relaxed. Usually, the first two or three months of an opening, I'm focused on all the details, not trusting 100 percent, always double-checking—until Coconut Grove. Today, I can confidently say the best way to do business is having the right people next to you. Now we do openings and everything goes smoothly; our team sees that I am much more relaxed. By the Aventura opening in 2022, I was a lot more relaxed because we did some great hiring there, and I knew we were set up

TOP: A dedicated server from the Pembroke Pines location.
Bottom: The manager, Lis, and Ana, from the iconic South Beach location.

TIME FOR
EXTRAORDINARY
PIZZA
WWW.MISTERO1.COM

for success. Even Grace, who has seen me go through so many openings, can admit that I have eased up a bit.

"Yes, he is more relaxed . . . but when he's onsite, the old chef comes out," says Grace. "But in the past, he would be there from open to close, all day during the opening months. Now he relies more on the team to handle it."

A group of front-of-house and back-of-house team members from the Fort Lauderdale and Lake Mary locations.

THE MISTER 01 PLAYLIST

The Mister O1 playlist, unaltered since our South Beach debut, consists of 58 timeless songs spanning 2 hours and 22 minutes. Boasting classic American hits predominantly from the 1950s. Our playlist encapsulates the essence of Mister O1's timeless ambiance.

Rockin' Robin
Bobby Day

Little Bitty Pretty One
Frankie Lymon

I Can't Help Myself (Sugar Pie Honey Bunch)
Four Tops

I Get Around
The Beach Boys

Surfin' Safari
The Beach Boys

Surfin' USA
The Beach Boys

Don't Be Cruel
Elvis Presley

Hound Dog
Elvis Presley

All Shook Up
Elvis Presley

(Let Me Be Your) Teddy Bear

Elvis Presley

Jail House Rock

Elvis Presley

Hard-Headed Woman

Elvis Presley

Stuck On You

Elvis Presley

Old Time Rock & Roll

Bob Seger & the Silver Bullet Band

Chantilly Lace

The Big Bopper

Rock Around the Clock

Bill Haley & His Comets

Splish Splash

Bobby Darin

Oh, Boy

Buddy Holly & the Crickets

Lollipop

The Chordettes

Tequila

The Champs

Let's Twist Again (Radio version)

Chubby Checker

Sweet Little Sixteen

Chuck Berry

My Babe

Dale Hawkins

At the Hop

Danny & The Juniors

Runaround Sue

Dion

Oh Lonesome Me

Don Gibson

Hello Josephine

Fats Domino

Tweedle Dee

Frankie Vaughn

Say Mama

Gene Vincent

Reet Petite

Jackie Wilson

Great Balls of Fire

Jerry Lee Lewis

Honeycomb

Jimmie Rodgers

Blue Moon

The Marcels

Hit the Road Jack

Ray Charles

Hello Mary Lou

Ricky Nelson

Drums a Go Go (Radio version)

Sandy Nelson

Let's Have a Party

Wanda Jackson

What'd I Say, Pt. 1

Ray Charles

Valerie (*Glee* Cast Season 5)

Glee Cast

I Got a Woman (Single)

Ray Charles

Anna Mae

Brownie McGhee

Hot Rod

Hal Singer and His Orchestra

Stop, Don't Go

Annie Laurie

Little By Little

Nappy Brown

Twist and Shout

The Isley Brothers

The Loco Motion

Little Eva

The Wanderer

Dion

Red Hot

Billy Lee Riley

Blue Suede Shoes

Elvis Presley

Tutti Frutti

Little Richard

Oh, Pretty Woman

Roy Orbison

Mess Around

Ray Charles

The Twist

Chubby Checker

Whole Lot of Shakin' Going On

Jerry Lee Lewis

NAVIGATING COVID

TOP: Chef Renato with guest and friend Romero Britto at the Coconut Grove location. BOTTOM: Chef Renato during COVID at the Wynwood location.

As mentioned earlier, we opened Coconut Grove in the midst of the COVID pandemic, after months of navigating the challenges it brought to our industry. When the world shut down in March of 2020, we never stopped operating. Though we closed our dining rooms, we continued to offer delivery, keeping a small team at each location to fulfill orders. We are proud to say that we never laid off anyone and kept everyone on payroll. This was a huge accomplishment for us, especially as we saw much larger hospitality companies lay off their employees and stop paying them.

The pandemic was one of the worst crises for the food and beverage industry, but we managed to survive for several reasons. The ability to continue delivery services and the popularity of pizza during the pandemic were key factors. Additionally, our well-structured organization and meticulous paperwork enabled us to quickly secure a PPP loan and keep paying our employees.

On a personal level, it was very hard not to be in contact with our guests. I remember walking into our empty Wynwood location during the shutdown and feeling incredibly sad. I was used to seeing people waiting outside, eager to dine with us. The city-mandated curfews added another layer of stress, as we had to ensure our employees left work in time to be home before curfew. We provided them with letters explaining their need to be out for work. The constant focus on social distancing and masking was challenging, and despite our best efforts to keep everyone safe, people inevitably got sick.

This was particularly significant during the opening of our Coconut Grove location. We needed all hands on deck, but many staff members called out sick with the virus. We had to pull staff from other locations and come together to ensure a great opening, which we achieved.

The pandemic was one of the worst crises for the food and beverage industry, but we managed to survive for several reasons. The ability to continue delivery services and the popularity of pizza during the pandemic were key factors.

An interesting development during COVID was that our friend Mimmo became a franchisee. His restaurant Dolce had closed, and he was looking for new opportunities in hospitality. He helped us with the Coconut Grove opening, which wouldn't have been possible without the COVID shutdown. During that time, he visited Melbourne, Florida, felt it was a good fit for the brand, and asked to open a location there. We trusted Mimmo and felt he was a good franchise partner, so we supported him in opening the Melbourne location in December 2021, which has been successful since.

Chef Renato and Mimmo, the franchise owner of the Melbourne location.

CHAPTER 6

THE MAGIC OF OUR MENU

OUR UNIQUE RECIPES

I won't claim that our pizza is better than anyone else's because taste is subjective. However, I will say that our pizza is unique. At Mister O1, you will always find something different. We prioritize using simple ingredients because we value speed in pizza preparation. We don't want our guests to wait too long, and this also helps in creating methods for our franchise partners.

We encourage people to try new things, and if they don't like it, they can send it back. We're always open to finding something fun and unexpected to replace it. Word of mouth is powerful for us, as people talk about our unique pizzas.

A great example is the Coffee Paolo pizza (page 109), which features tomato sauce, ground coffee, blue cheese, honey, and spicy Calabrian salami. I dreamed of this pizza one night, wrote it down, and began experimenting until I found the perfect combination. It was approved by President and Manuela and has since become a popular, buzz-worthy menu item that appeals to food writers.

THE DOUGH

The secret to our pizza is the flour, not necessarily the dough. Our flour is made from a special type of grain with higher protein content, sourced from a farm in Italy. It's natural, non-GMO, and mixed in a customized way. This gives our dough its signature taste and texture. I prefer Italian flours because American flours are not always consistent.

We also offer a gluten-free dough made with rice flour, which is light and easy to digest. To ensure consistency, I created specific software to measure and mix the flour accurately. Timing, temperature, and ingredient proportions are all crucial factors that need to be controlled. The dough must be 71 to 73 degrees Fahrenheit (22 to 23 degrees Celsius) when finished to avoid premature gluten cooking.

In 2017, we moved our dough production to the Wynwood location, investing in a spiral mixer that doubled our production capacity. We also purchased equipment to help with the dough process, allowing us to make 300 dough balls an hour. Each dough ball is matured for a minimum of 72 hours, up to 140 hours. Our dough is now made in an 8,000-square-foot commissary kitchen and delivered to all our Florida locations, enabling them to create 700 pizzas a day.

The Coffee Paolo pizza (page 109) made with our gluten-free crust option.

THE DOUGH

Thin crust
Makes 7 (13-inch) pizzas

INGREDIENTS:

900 g/ 31.75 oz Flour
2g/ 0.07 oz Yeast
500 ml water
25g/ 0.88 oz Salt
25g/ 0.88 oz Extra Virgin Olive Oil

STEP BY STEP:

- Put the flour into a bowl.
- Add yeast to the flour and mix well.
- Add the water.
- Hold the bowl with one hand and use the other hand to knead the dough until the water is fully absorbed by the flour.
- Once the dough is formed, add the salt in two equal parts to make sure it is evenly blended.
- Add the olive oil and knead it into the dough.
- Take out the dough from the bowl and move onto a clean surface table. Scrape the bowl clean so no dough is wasted.
- Knead the dough by pressing and rotating for about 10 minutes to develop the gluten. The dough is ready when it does not stick to the table.
- Cover the dough with plastic wrap and let sit for 10 minutes.
- After letting it rest, divide it with a scraper into pieces of 200 grams each.
- Grab each individual piece, and gently shape it into a ball by hand.
- Put the pieces in a foil pan and refrigerate.

STAR LUCA (page 107)
CLAUDIO

COFFEE PAOLO (page 109)

STAR LUCA

Makes (1) 13-inch pizza

INGREDIENTS:

1.5 oz tomato sauce
2.8 oz mozzarella cheese
18–20 pieces spicy salami calabrese
200 g ricotta (25 g, or 0.9 oz, for each pocket)
0.5 oz basil

STEP BY STEP:

- Preheat oven to 320 degrees Fahrenheit.
- Stretch a large dough into a 13-inch circle.
- Make 8 equidistant 1-inch cuts around the edge of the dough using a small pizza wheel cutter.
- Spoon half a ladle of tomato sauce and spread evenly over the dough in a circular motion from the center to the cuts.
- Spread mozzarella cheese evenly over the sauce, making sure not to use too much cheese.
- Top the pizza with slices of spicy salami, making sure to get salami in the 8 corners of the star as well as in the center area.
- Pipe ricotta cheese on the 8 flaps of the star, 25 grams on each flap for 200 grams in total.
- Begin to close the star by bringing together two edges and pinching the dough to form each point.
- Bake the pizza until the crust is crisp and golden brown.
- Remove from the oven and place on a plate. Cut the pizza into 8 even slices using a pizza wheel cutter. Garnish with chiffonade basil.

COFFEE PAOLO

Makes (1) 13-inch pizza

INGREDIENTS:

3 oz tomato sauce
3.5 oz mozzarella cheese
1.8 oz Gorgonzola blue cheese
18–20 pieces of spicy salami calabrese
1.2 oz natural honey
0.2 oz ground coffee

STEP BY STEP:

- Preheat oven to 320 degrees Fahrenheit.
- Stretch the large dough into a 13-inch circle.
- Spoon one ladle of tomato sauce and spread evenly over the dough in a circular motion, making sure to leave a half inch border on the outside.
- Top with mozzarella cheese to evenly coat the surface of the dough, making sure not to use too much cheese.
- Add Gorgonzola blue cheese evenly.
- Top the pizza with 20 pieces of spicy salami.
- Drizzle the honey evenly on top of the pizza.
- Bake the pizza util the crust is crisp and golden brown.
- Remove from the oven and place on a plate.
- Cut the pizza into 6 even slices using a pizza wheel cutter.
- Sprinkle ground coffee evenly over the pizza.

Extraordinary
Mister01

ANCHOVY BOTTARGA GIAMPAOLO

STRACCIATELLA AND BURRATA

We are very proud of our stracciatella and burrata cheeses. Stracciatella, made from pulled mozzarella curds mixed with fresh cream, is the gooey interior of burrata. Burrata has an outer casing of solid cheese with a soft, creamy interior. These cheeses are made by a family-run factory in Miami using milk from Wisconsin. They use no preservatives, and the burrata lasts only ten days, compared to twenty-two days for commercially available burratas.

We specify a creamier stracciatella for our pizzas, which we spread on the pizza as soon as it comes out of the oven. This technique brings down the pizza's temperature, enhancing the flavor and creaminess of the cheese. We educate our guests about this method, as it sometimes surprises them that the pizza is not served hot.

When we opened a franchise in Texas, we couldn't find the right quality of stracciatella and burrata locally. To maintain our standards, we ship the cheese to Texas every other day. In each city, we adapt to local tastes, like using a local sausage in Texas.

We emphasize our commitment to quality ingredients from Italy. In the beginning, we spent a lot of time explaining our ingredients to guests. Now, pizza is seen as a culinary experience and is artisanal. We adapt to local preferences, such as evolving from thicker to thinner pizza dough.

Rocco, owner of Capri Organic, leading a cheese class and explaining the process of making Burrata.

BURRATA

Serves 2

INGREDIENTS:

3 slices of tomato
1 (4 oz) burrata ball
extra virgin olive oil
oregano
salt
black pepper
1.5 oz arugula

STEP BY STEP:

- Place three slices of tomato on one half of the board.
- Place the burrata ball on top of the tomato slices.
- Garnish the burrata with a half ounce of olive oil, and a pinch of oregano, salt, and pepper.
- In a mixing bowl, add the arugula and season with a pinch of salt and a drizzle of olive oil.
- Toss the arugula to coat evenly.
- Place the arugula on the other half of the board.
- Serve with a side of warm focaccia bread (see recipe on page 116).

Spicy
Extra Virgin
Olive Oil
COLD PRESSED
FIRST PRESS
8.5 us fl oz (250 ml)

FOCACCIA

Serves 2

INGREDIENTS:

1 dough ball
1 sprig rosemary
0.25 oz extra virgin olive oil
1 pinch salt

STEP BY STEP:

- Preheat oven to 320 degrees Fahrenheit.
- Stretch the pizza dough to approximately 12 inches.
- Place a sprig of rosemary in the center.
- Drizzle the dough with the extra virgin olive oil and sprinkle lightly with salt.
- Poke holes in the dough and place in the oven.
- Bake until golden brown spots appear on the surface and the dough is completely cooked.
- Remove and cut into 8 strips.
- Stack the strips and place into a brown paper bag with the rosemary on top.
- Serve it with the burrata (see page 115).

PIZZA CLAUDIO WITH MISTER 01 TRUFFLE OIL

CAESAR SALAD

Serves 2

INGREDIENTS:

4–6 handfuls (14 oz) chopped romaine
3.1 oz Caesar dressing, plus more for drizzle
1.75 oz croutons
1.4 oz shaved Parmesan

STEP BY STEP:

- Place the chopped romaine in a mixing bowl.
- Add the Caesar dressing to the romaine lettuce.
- Using gloves, mix the lettuce by hand to dress and evenly coat all the romaine lettuce.
- Empty the tossed romaine into a salad bowl.
- Top with croutons.
- Garnish with shaved Parmesan cheese and drizzle caesar dressing on top to garnish.
- Serve with tongs.

MARCO

Makes (1) 13-inch pizza

INGREDIENTS:

1 regular dough
3 oz tomato sauce
5.2 oz stracciatella cheese
1.2 oz arugula
2 oz diced tomatoes
1 oz shaved Parmesan
0.5 oz extra virgin olive oil

STEP BY STEP:

- Preheat oven to 320 degrees Fahrenheit.
- Stretch the large dough into a 13-inch circle.
- Spoon one ladle of tomato sauce and spread evenly over the dough in a circular motion, making sure to leave a half-inch border on the outside.
- Bake the pizza util the crust is crisp and golden brown.
- Remove from the oven and place on a plate.
- Pour one portion container of stracciatella in the center of the baked pizza.
- Spread the stracciatella evenly to cover the entire surface of the pizza.
- Cut the pizza into six even slices using a pizza wheel cutter.
- Top the pizza with arugula, diced tomatoes, and Parmesan cheese.
- Drizzle extra virgin olive oil on top to finish.

HONORING OUR GUESTS

We pay tribute to our guests by naming pizzas after them. Here are some of our special creations and the people who inspired them:

These names reflect the personal connections and stories that make Mister O1 special. Our pizzas are not just meals; they are tributes to the people who have supported and inspired us along the way.

STAR LUCA: Named after one of my good friends (page 107).

GINGER LILLIAM: Created for a loyal guests' wife. The guest gave us a blank check to do whatever we wanted, and we created this pizza featuring fresh ginger, black pepper, and stracciatella. It's only available in South Beach.

STAR LAINA: Named after our first franchisee. Available in Naples, Ft. Lauderdale, Melbourne, Boca Raton, and all Texas locations. Made with ricotta, Parmesan, and garlic.

STAR ALEJANDRO: In honor of franchisee Alejandro. Available in Pembroke Pines, Boca Raton and Orlando. Made with corn, ham, and white truffle.

CLAUDIO: Named for our good friend and lawyer who has been with us since day one.

FEDERICA: Created for one of our first guests, whose kids have been eating my pizza for ten years. Made with black olives, ham, and mushroom.

MARCO: A tribute to a friend who has always been by my side during good times and bad (page 125).

STAR CARLOS: Dedicated to Carlos Galan, a Spanish restaurateur. Made with chorizo, arugula, and jalapeno sauce (page 129).

ALESSANDRA JALAPENO: Inspired by a pizza class attendee who made the most original pizza. Features jalapeno, mushroom, and avocado.

STAR BECKHAM: Named after the famous soccer player. Initially called Star David, but he requested it be named Star Beckham for the whole family. They all enjoy dining with us.

SABRINA: Named after a former boss of my wife when she worked in a clothing store.

STAR CARLOS

Makes (1) 13-inch pizza

INGREDIENTS:

1 dough ball
3.2 oz mozzarella cheese
16 pieces (2 oz) chorizo sausage
200 g ricotta (25 g/0.9 oz for each pocket)
1 oz arugula, chopped
2 oz diced tomatoes, chopped
1/2 (2 oz) avocado, chopped
0.5 oz jalapeno sauce
0.7 oz shaved Parmesan

STEP BY STEP:

- Preheat oven to 320 degrees Fahrenheit.
- Stretch a large dough into a 13-inch circle.
- Make 8 equidistant 1-inch cuts around the edge of the dough using a small pizza wheel cutter.
- Spread mozzarella cheese evenly over the sauce, making sure not to use too much cheese.
- Top the pizza with small pieces of chorizo sausage, ensuring that we have chorizo in all 8 corners of the star, as well as in the center.
- Pipe ricotta cheese on the 8 flaps of the star, 25 grams on each flap, for 200 grams in total.
- Begin to close the star by bringing together two edges and pinching the dough to form 8 points.
- Bake pizza until the crust is crisp and golden brown.
- Remove from the oven and place on a plate.
- Cut into 8 equal slices using a pizza wheel cutter
- In a mixing bowl, add the arugula, tomatoes, and chopped avocado. Toss them in the jalapeńo sauce.
- Spread the prepared salad on the pizza and evenly cover the surface. Top it with shaved Parmesan.

NUTELLA PIZZA

NUTELLA PIZZA

Makes (1) 13-inch pizza

INGREDIENTS:

1 dough ball
4.6 oz Nutella
0.3 oz powdered sugar

STEP BY STEP:

- Preheat oven to 320 degrees Fahrenheit.
- Stretch the large dough into a 13-inch circle
- Poke holes in the dough to prevent the dough from puffing up.
- Bake the dough until just cooked. Do not let the dough brown too much or get too crisp.
- Flip the dough over onto a plate
- Using a spoon, scoop Nutella onto the center of the warm dough.
- Spread nutella with the spoon on the baked dough to form a thin even layer.
- Cut the pizza into 6 equal slices using a small pizza cutter.
- Dust the nutella with powdered sugar.

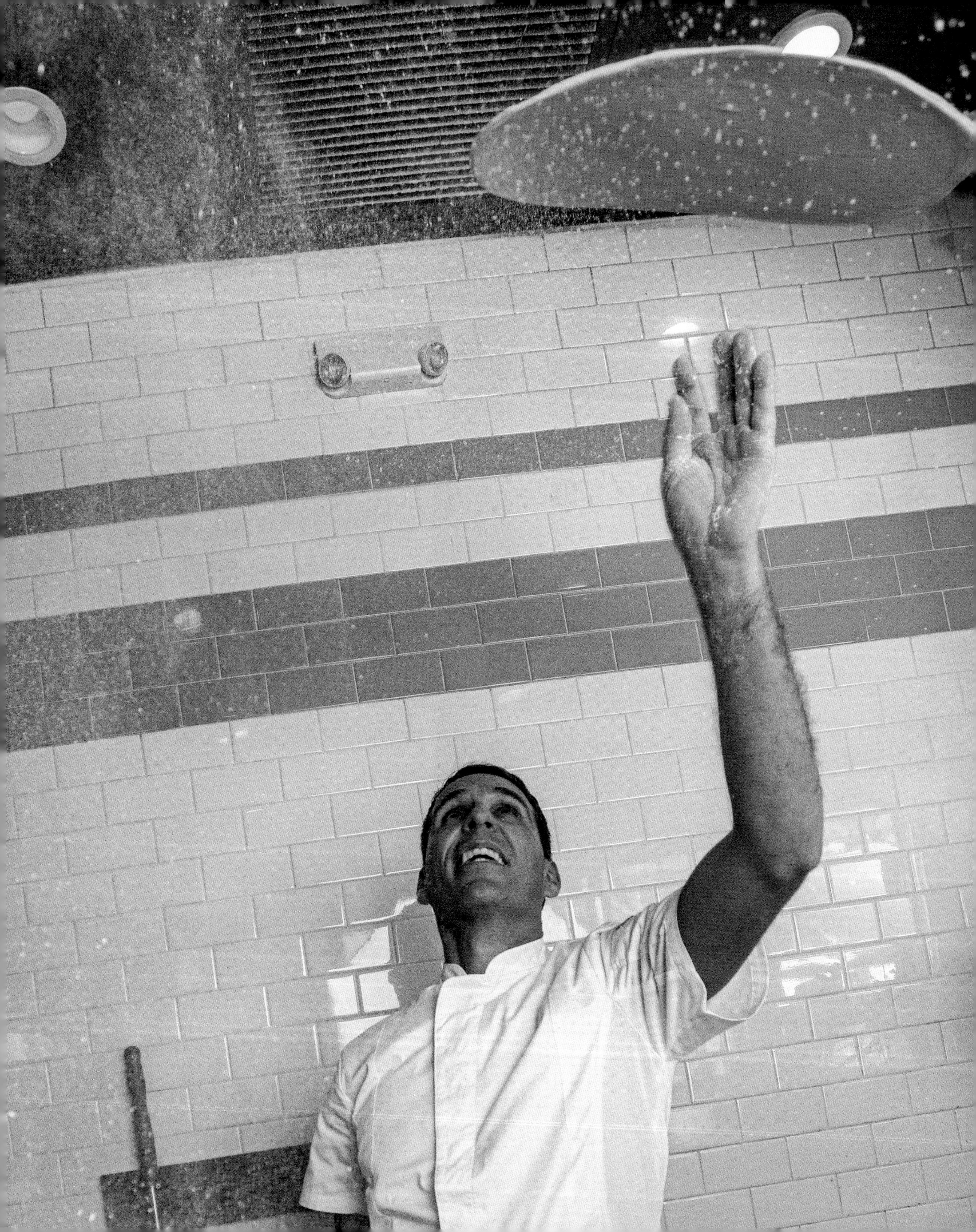

CHAPTER 7

EMBARKING ON A FRACHISE PLAN

STREAMLINING THE PROCESS

One day while I was at the Brickell location, a tall man named Larry Petit asked to speak with the owner—me. He expressed his vision for franchising Mister O1. Representing a company that evaluates business franchisability, he believed our brand had great potential. Initially skeptical, I thanked him for his time. However, as more people approached us with similar ideas each week, we began to see the merit in the concept. We decided to create a Franchise Disclosure Document (FDD), providing comprehensive information for potential franchisees.

After granting Larry access to all our numbers, we eagerly awaited his assessment. Six weeks later, he delivered the news we had hoped for—Mister O1 was indeed a viable franchise brand. We hired Larry to represent us and help identify the right franchise partners. He assisted in creating essential materials, from construction manuals to marketing collateral, streamlining the franchising process.

Preparing these materials took a year, during which Larry interviewed numerous individuals interested in franchising with us. However, many were investors lacking operational experience, not aligned with our brand vision. Then, our South Beach chef mentioned a woman named Laina who expressed regular interest in franchising. Impressed by her extensive management and marketing expertise, along with her passion for our brand, we were immediately sold.

After three months of discussions, we signed a contract with Laina for the first Mister O1 franchise. In March 2019, she successfully opened in Naples, marking the beginning of her journey with the brand, followed by Fort Lauderdale in January 2023. Laina is now actively building her second location in South Naples while also exploring opportunities for further growth in other areas of Broward County.

Franchisees often seek to expand once they experience success. The group behind our Boca Raton location

TOP: Chef Renato with Texas Franchise Operating Partner John LaBarge.
ABOVE: Naples and Fort Lauderdale Franchise Owner Laina Kennedy.
OPPOSITE, TOP: AKA Group Daniel Cohen on the left and Alberto Strulovic on the right (Texas, Orlando, and Boca Raton).
OPPOSITE, BOTTOM: Franchise Owner Alejandro Ciffoni, and his business partner, Marines Smith (Pembroke Pines).

1680

1680

The dining room at the Pembroke Pines location.

As a brand, we believe in franchising but prioritize quality partnerships.

eventually acquired rights for the entire state of Texas. It all began with Alejandro Ciffoni, a Mister O1 enthusiast who, along with his partner Marines Smith, approached us about opening a location in Broward County.

Though Alejandro had a background in professional tennis, his management experience and infectious energy won us over. With the help of a consulting firm, he identified Pembroke Pines and Miramar as ideal locations. Daniel, the head of the consulting company, later became our franchisee in Boca Raton and expanded into Texas.

Despite owning multiple franchises, Daniel had never encountered a concept aligned with our quality-focused mindset. He, along with partners Alberto and Andres, opened the Boca Raton location near Mizner Park, serving as a testament to the concept's success. They secured Palm Beach County and are now expanding into Northern Florida and Texas.

As a brand, we believe in franchising but prioritize quality partnerships. We reject offers from individuals lacking operational experience, even if financially sound. Aggressive expansion plans, like opening seventy-five locations in three years, are also turned down if deemed unsuitable. Additionally, we avoid food halls and overcrowding pizza markets, maintaining final approval to safeguard our brand integrity.

Mimmo further articulates our franchise philosophy: "We are a franchise but not a chain; it's not about investors putting in money and stepping away. Chef Renato prefers gradual growth, ensuring operators are deeply invested in and passionate about the brand."

TIMELINE/MILESTONES

Grateful for Every Community That Welcomes Mister O1

OCTOBER 21, 2014 South Beach

OCTOBER 13, 2016 Brickell

OCTOBER 4, 2017 Wynwood

March 12, 2019 Naples (Franchise)

JANUARY 19, 2021 Coconut Grove

MARCH 1, 2022 Boca Raton (Franchise)

MARCH 29, 2022 Aventura

MAY 2, 2023 Grapevine, TX (Franchise)

OCTOBER 17, 2023 Bay Harbor Islands

APRIL 9, 2024 Flower Mound, TX (Franchise)

APRIL 23, 2024 Mission Bay (Franchise)

DECEMBER 14, 2021 Melbourne (Franchise)

FEBRUARY 1, 2022 Pembroke Pines (Franchise)

OCTOBER 11, 2022 Dallas, TX (Franchise)

JANUARY 3, 2023 Fort Lauderdale (Franchise)

NOVEMBER 7, 2023 Lake Mary (Franchise)

NOVEMBER 14, 2023 Mansfield, TX (Franchise)

JUNE 25, 2024 Pinecrest

SEPTEMBER 24, 2024 Dr. Philips (Franchise)

CUPPON

CHAPTER 8

THE ESSENCE OF DESIGN

CRAFTING A WELCOMING SPACE

Our design philosophy has remained unwaveringly simple since the inception of Mister O1 in South Beach a decade ago. Our aim was to craft a welcoming space where guests could feel at ease. Opting for butcher block tables was a deliberate choice; for me, wood embodies life itself. In every establishment, we showcase an open kitchen—the heart of the operation. The oven and pizzeria serve as the stage; transparency is key, as we have nothing to conceal. I take pride in being a pizza chef and relish interacting with our guests.

During our inaugural venture, we personally crafted the floor design using chalk. Lacking a kitchen designer, we prioritized the kitchen layout. I meticulously planned the kitchen and pizza station to ensure optimal performance and ample space for the team. Contrary to conventional wisdom, which often favors maximizing dining space over kitchen size, we prioritize functionality. Our goal is efficiency, hence the inclusion of two ovens capable of producing one hundred pizzas each per hour. Cooking around twelve pizzas simultaneously for three to four minutes, our setup ensures prompt service. The salad station is equally pivotal, comprising one of three primary stations alongside pizza stretching and toppings, and oven operations. On busy nights, up to eleven chefs may man these stations. Notably, we eschew fryers and refrain from incorporating sugar into the dough or sauce.

Embracing the notion of communal dining, we sought flexibility in table arrangements. Employing 1.5-inch thick butcher block tables measuring 28 by 25 inches, we facilitate easy reconfiguration for larger parties. Bench seating and booths are absent from our design ethos, as they restrict flexibility. Our signage and branding graphics, conceptualized by our longstanding friend Mitico in Italy, exude elegance and remain unchanged since our inception.

Our aim was to craft a welcoming space where guests could feel at ease.

ABOVE: Interior of the Lake Mary location.
OPPOSITE, TOP: Interior of the Bay Harbor location.
OPPOSITE, BOTTOM: Interior of the Turtle Creek location—first Mister O1 in Texas.

Embracing the notion of communal dining, we sought flexibility in table arrangements.

Bench seating and booths are absent from our design ethos, as they restrict flexibility.

Music plays an integral role in our design scheme. We believe that every detail contributes to a lasting memory, from the aroma to the visuals. With an unwavering focus on acoustics, we've maintained the same playlist for a decade. Featuring American rock classics from the 1950s Our playlist sets the tone for the Mister O1 experience. Despite occasional suggestions for change, we stand firm; the playlist is non-negotiable, emblematic of our brand identity. Transparency extends to our franchisees, with very few aspects open for negotiation.

The back-of-house team at work in the open kitchen of the Grapevine location.

TOP: The service station, Turtle Creek location.
BOTTOM: The open kitchen concept, Mansfield location.

The dining room at the Mansfield location.

EXIT
Individuals with extraordinary ability.
To qualify for an O-1 visa in the US,
the beneficiary must demonstrate extraordinary
ability by sustained national or international acclaim.

LOCATIONS

MisterO1
BRICKELL
PIZZA, SALADS &
BURRATA BAR
DINE IN, TAKEOUT & DELIVERY
MISTER 01
900 S MIAMI AVE, SUITE #130
MIAMI, FL 33130
@MISTER01PIZZA
MISTER01.COM
RETAIL

SOUTH BEACH, FLORIDA (2014)
1680 Michigan Ave, Suite #101
Miami Beach, FL 33139

BRICKELL, FLORIDA (2016)
900 S Miami Ave, Suite #130
Miami, FL 33130

WYNWOOD, FLORIDA (2017)
2315 N Miami Ave
Miami, FL 33127

NAPLES, FLORIDA (2019)
2355 Vanderbilt Beach Rd, Suite #176
Naples, FL 34109

COCONUT GROVE, FLORIDA (2021)
3015 Grand Ave, Suite #165
Miami, FL 33133

MELBOURNE, FLORIDA (2021)
635 E New Haven Ave, Suite #101
Melbourne, FL 32901

PEMBROKE PINES, FLORIDA (2022)
10640 Pines Blvd, Suite #F101
Pembroke Pines, FL 33026

BOCA RATON, FLORIDA (2022)
555 N Federal Hwy, Suite #5
Boca Raton, FL 33432

AVENTURA, FLORIDA (2022)
2980 NE 207th St, Suite #109
Aventura, FL 33180

DALLAS, TEXAS (2022)
3838 Oak Lawn Ave, Suite #P175
Dallas, TX 75219

FORT LAUDERDALE, FLORIDA (2023)
415 NE 4th St
Fort Lauderdale, FL 33301

GRAPEVINE, TEXAS (2023)
129 S Main St, Suite #155
Grapevine, TX 76051

BAY HARBOR, FLORIDA (2023)
1065 95th Street
Bay Harbor Islands, FL 33154

LAKE MARY, FLORIDA (2023)
1210 S International Pkwy, Suite #108
Heathrow, FL 32746

MANSFIELD, TEXAS (2023)
1520 E Debbie Ln, Suite #102
Mansfield, TX 76063

FLOWER MOUND, TEXAS (2024)
4630 Long Prairie Rd, Suite #220
Flower Mound, TX 75028

MISSION BAY, FLORIDA (2024)
20401 FL-7, Suite #G-4
Boca Raton, FL 33498

PINECREST, FLORIDA (2024)
8189 SW 117th St
Pinecrest, FL 33156

DR. PHILLIPS (2024)
7541 W Sand Lake Rd, Suite D
Orlando, FL 32819

BOYNTON BEACH (2024)
7381 Boynton Beach Blvd, Suite #305
Boynton Beach, FL 33437

DORAL (2024)
8455 NW 53rd St, G101
Doral, FL 33166

ABOUT THE CHEF

Renato Viola is the co-founder and head chef of Mister 01 Extraordinary Pizza, a celebrated pizzeria based in Miami. His passion for pizza-making began in his childhood kitchen, where he honed his skills under the guidance of his mother and grandmother. This early inspiration sparked a lifelong journey that would lead him to join the prestigious Italian Pizza Acrobatic Team and become a celebrated figure in the pizza-making world.

Chef Renato's career took him across Europe, where he earned numerous accolades, including the coveted title of "Best Pizza" at the Pizza World Championship for his iconic Star Luca pizza. He also holds a Guinness World Record for creating the "Most Expensive Pizza in the World" and was recognized as one of the "Top 50 Executives" in the Top 100 Movers & Shakers by *Pizza Marketplace*.

Born in Southern Italy, Chef Renato eventually brought his talents to the United States, where he co-founded Mister 01. The restaurant has quickly gained a reputation for its creative, high-quality pizzas, expanding to over twenty locations across the country, including south and central Florida, Naples, Florida, and Dallas Texas. Mister 01 has received numerous accolades, including being named the "Best Pizza in Florida" by *Food & Wine* magazine and earning a spot on the Michelin Guide's recommended list. The pizzeria was also recognized as "Best Pizza" by the *Miami New Times* for three consecutive years.

Chef Renato's dedication to innovation and quality continues to drive Mister 01's success, attracting a loyal following in his hometown, Miami, and beyond.

ACKNOWLEDGMENTS

As we reflect on the journey that has brought us to where we are today—with the creation and growth of Mister O1—we are filled with deep gratitude. This book, much like the pizza we create, is the result of countless ingredients: hard work, passion, inspiration, and, most importantly, the incredible support we've received along the way.

To our franchise partners, thank you for believing in this vision and for helping us grow beyond what we could have imagined. Your trust and collaboration have been integral to our success, and together we've created something truly special.

To our entire Mister O1 team, both in the kitchen and front-of-house—thank you. Your hard work, passion, and tireless effort are the foundation of this brand. You bring our vision to life every single day, and for that, we are endlessly grateful.

We are also deeply grateful to our suppliers, vendors, and partners for providing the highest-quality ingredients and exceptional products. Your support elevates the Mister O1 experience and is a vital part of our continued success.

To our distributors, publisher, and author—thank you for your invaluable contributions in bringing this story to life. Your professionalism, creativity, and support have been pivotal in making this project a reality.

Finally, to our guests, thank you from the bottom of our hearts. You are the soul of Mister O1. Your love for what we create, your loyalty, and your belief in us mean everything. You've welcomed us into your lives and made us part of your most special moments.

This journey has been nothing short of extraordinary. As we continue to innovate and open new doors, we carry the contributions of every person who has been part of this story with us. Thank you for your support, love, and inspiration. Here's to the next extraordinary chapter.

With all our gratitude,
Renato and Umberto

Mister O1
Mister O1
Extraordinary
Pizza

1680

MisterO1
Extraordinary
Pizza